To A
GREAT DENTIST
AND A
GOOD FRIEND

Jack Epstein

Adventures with Jack

Stories to Make You Smile

Jack Epstein

Acorn Press
Winchester, Virginia

Dedication

I dedicate this book with love to three women
who have played important parts in my life:
my late sister, Freda Epstein Hecht,
my late wife, Ruth Gutman Epstein,
and my dear friend, Mary Sarin Covan.

Acknowledgments

This book would not have been possible without the love and support of a number of my friends. I would like to thank the late Bob Griffiths for his contribution to this effort, and Nick Samadge, photographer, for his assistance with the photographs.

Also, thanks to Joyce Gioia for her help in editing and otherwise preparing this manuscript for publication, and to Carol Neuman, who had a hand in final preparation.

Disclaimer

At the age of 93, as of this writing, I hereby inform you that I did not keep a journal or a diary. All of the stories in this book were accessed from my memory that may not be perfect. Also, be advised that when memory failed, I took license to fill in the important names and dates.

Introduction

In accordance with my wishes, my most valued friends will receive a copy of this collection of some of my most treasured memories. Many of these incidents were pivotal in my life and added that extra bit of zest that is so important to one's outlook and enjoyment of life.

I can't give you a reason why I wanted to write this book. Call it "ego," call it "joy of authorship," or maybe, "just for laughs." Whatever the reason, I hope you will derive at least a smile from some of these rather amusing incidents in the life of one Jack Epstein.

Table of Contents

Table of Contents

Table of Contents

Table of Contents

Always Leave Them Laughing

One of the main interests in my life has always been animals. I enjoy reading about them, watching them on the screen, and visiting the various zoos around the country. During my teen years, a friend of my father got me a "helper job" in the Baltimore Zoo. I cleaned the cages, carried the feed buckets, and hosed down the animals.

One rule was strictly enforced and taught to each new zoo employee: if you go into a cage alone, always carry a long handled broom. Once you were inside the cage, the animals' eyes focused on the broom and not you directly.

One day with feed bucket in hand, I entered the polar bears' cage. There were two bear inhabitants—one huge male bear and a female bear that was almost as large. They didn't intimidate me, but rest assured, I kept my broom directly in front of their view.

After placing the feed bucket on the ground, and still swinging the broom, I slowly backed towards the door. All of a sudden, the male bear sprung with one quick move and with one swipe sent the long handled broom to the top of the twenty foot ceiling.

However, instead of making me the next victim, the big bear sat back on his haunches and laughed like crazy. The female soon joined in. Bears *do* laugh, soundlessly, with their heads thrown back and tongues out. Suddenly, I felt like Bob Hope.

I emerged from this traumatic experience unscathed. To add icing on the cake, from that day on I was a welcome visitor to the polar bear cage—without my broom. Those crazy bears had a perverted sense of humor.

Take Me Out of the Ball Game

You never know when circumstances can quickly make you a hero. A case in point: I was fourteen years of age and attending Camp Kennebec in Maine. I played center field on the baseball team. Not well, but passably.

It was our big game. The next hitter up was anything but a heavy hitter, so I was playing close in on him in center field. As luck would have it, he connected with a fast ball and sent it screaming right at me. I lunged for the liner and misjudged it. The ball caught me squarely in the midsection. I felt as though I had been hit with a cannon ball. However, I did hang on to the ball.

Momentarily stunned, I staggered forward and fell on second base—just in time to double off a runner completing a double play. This play retired the other side, and we won the game.

That night at the banquet, I was given the award for the best play of the game. Frankly, I was looking for something more appropriate—like a shot of liniment for my aching stomach.

Monkey Business

One of the more pleasant jobs I had with the Baltimore Zoo was feeding the monkeys. There were about fifty of them in the enclosure and each day they awaited my arrival with their food.

We had a daily routine we followed to the letter. This routine mandated that one monkey, Jocko, by name, should always be fed first—then the others followed. Upon my arrival in the Monkey House, I would stand for a minute until Jocko appeared and climbed up my leg and body until he hugged me around the neck. Then he was fed and afterwards, the others would receive their dinner. This little rite played out daily for several months.

One day, however, Jocko didn't appear immediately at dinnertime. Another little fellow scooted up my body and hugged me around the neck, following Jocko's routine.

Just as I was about to feed him, I felt a tug and there was Jocko, in a fit of rage, climbing up my leg. Needless to say, the other monkey made a hasty retreat. I could tell Jocko was furious. When he reached my arms, he dug into the fleshy part with his fingernails and gave me quite a clawing. My arm started to bleed profusely. But before I could dash to the dispensary, Jocko jumped on my shoulder and gave me a big hug, as if to apologize. I could tell by the look in his eyes the rage had disappeared, and he was trying to tell me how sorry he was for hurting me.

Someone once said mankind evolved from the apes. After this little incident, I am convinced we share many similar emotions—one being jealousy. I learned not to "monkey around" with this emotion ever again.

A Rose by Any Other Name

You should have known my mother. What a delightful character! To describe her is to run the gamut of adjectives. For starters, let me say that she was an opinionated, plain spoken, shoot-from-the-hip type of woman with deep insight, tempered with mercy and compassion.

For example: It was one of those warm and sunny days in New York. Mother was going with the flow of humanity crowding the sidewalks of Fifth Avenue. Suddenly, from out of the crush, a voice called out, "Aunt Laura, what a surprise!"

Taken aback, mother quickly turned to identify the voice that belonged to Margaret, an old friend of mine. What was more surprising to my mother was the fact that Margaret, a lesbian, was completely outfitted in men's clothing—fedora, shirt, tie, jacket, and slacks.

As the brief encounter ended, Margaret asked how she could get in touch with me. Without skipping a beat, mother told her she didn't know and that she hadn't heard from me in quite some time.

When I learned of this little incident a few days later, I was amazed at mother's response to the question about my whereabouts since we talked on the telephone almost daily. Her reply: "Do you think I'd tell that mannish-looking woman where *my* son was? Never!"

Fit to Be Tied

I am sure you have heard of Hollywood's famous Brown Derby Restaurant. For many years, it was the place to see and be seen. The food was fairly good, but the ambiance was always outstanding.

Anyway, Kathy and I decided to dress up and have dinner at the Brown Derby. I met Kathy at her door and she was a sight to behold—dressed in a chic little black "number" with gold accessories and an upswept hairdo. I, too, felt as if I had just stepped out of the pages of *GQ* Magazine with my blue blazer, white slacks, and a fairly expensive, open-neck, California sportshirt.

We arrived at our destination right on time for our reservation. We politely waited at the front of the restaurant for the maître'd to greet us. But, with one jaundiced look, he ceremoniously announced he couldn't seat us because I wasn't wearing a necktie.

His remark cut me to the quick. I had paid "big bucks" for this sportshirt and now it wouldn't pass muster at the Brown Derby. A slight hassle ensued but, not wanting to ruin Kathy's evening, I agreed to give the maître'd $5.00 for a necktie.

I must admit that the evening—comprised of a relaxed cocktail hour, gracious dining, and romantic dance music—was an unmitigated success. When it came time to go, Kathy and I headed for the door but were suddenly confronted by my "friend" the maître'd. He requested the return of "his" tie. I replied emphatically, "No way." As far as I was concerned, the $5.00 I gave him for the tie was a "sale." The tie was mine.

My "friend" was still protesting that the tie was merely a loan. Not wanting to cause a scene, I offered to sell the tie back to him for $5.00. Begrudgingly, the maître'd angrily gave me $5.00.

Looking back, I often wondered if the maître'd ever experienced a more exasperating confrontation. I bct he kept our little run-in under his hat— or should I say, "Derby?"

A Night in Casablanca

I agreed to accompany my dear friend, Mary, with other friends on a trip to Morocco. I shall never forget our special night in Casablanca. We went out to dinner with a group of Americans, most of whom could best be described as "stuffed shirts." We were bored. As we looked around the room, we discovered a large table of fun-loving Spaniards next to ours.

Not wanting to appear rude, we sat with our group. Mary excused herself from the table and was gone a very long time. I thought that she was in the ladies room, so I wasn't worried.

Suddenly, the band struck up a boisterous tune, the curtains parted, and there was Mary leading a conga line of rowdy Spaniards—all of whom were having a wonderful time! We spent the balance of the evening attempting to communicate with our new friends. The men were enthralled with Mary, and in spite of the language barrier, the women were wonderful dance partners.

An otherwise boring evening was turned into a night of fun and frolic, thanks to my delightful friend, Mary.

Jack and his friend, Mary, on the town

The Proper Introduction

My sister, Freda, was a great one for teaching her children manners. When Susan, her daughter, was about two or three years old, Freda thought it would be good for her child to get used to animals. She decided to get Susan a dog.

Freda asked me to be there when she introduced the new cocker spaniel, Tommy, to Susan. I told Freda I thought a formal introduction was in order.

Freda said, "Susan, I'd like you to meet Tommy."

As I held Tommy's paw and Freda held out Susan's right hand, I said, "Tommy, I'd like you to meet Susan."

The two shook hands. It went very well, until Susan, looking lovingly at her new friend, asked, "Tommy, what's your last name?"

Dowsing: It's Not Just for Water Anymore

A woman I'll call Alrume had not been feeling well for a couple of years. No physician had been able to diagnose her malady. She came to me, and asked if I could help her with my dowsing abilities (see the appendix for a complete explanation of "dowsing.")

I agreed to try to help. She arrived at my apartment soon thereafter. I used my pendulum to evaluate every part of her body. Just below the collarbone on the left side of her body, I found something radically wrong. I explained that I was not a medical doctor, but that I had found a serious condition that required immediate care.

It was then that she shared with me that she had an artificial heart valve in that area. I counselled her to see a doctor as soon as possible.

He discovered that the valve had become blocked. She was operated on immediately. Her life was saved.

It made me feel wonderful to know that I had made a difference in this woman's life.

The Pendulum Finds the Ring

Mildred was a good friend of my late wife Ruth. Ruth had told Mildred many times of my dowsing abilities. Mildred was very skeptical about the things that she had heard. However, one evening she invited Ruth and me for dinner and at one point said archly, "If you are so good, can you find my wedding ring that I lost two years ago?"

"Mildred," I said, "I'll see what I can do, but I must have a complete drawing and layout of every closet, room, and drawer in your apartment, and it must be accurate."

Much to my amazement, she did a very thorough job of drawing the apartment in detail.

A week later, she called Ruth and said that her skepticism was justified. She had not heard from me.

I called Mildred back and told her there were no time limits that I had to observe. Then, three weeks later at 3AM, I saw where Mildred's ring had been resting.

I called her and told her to look in the second closet on the right as she came into her apartment and go back to the rear where she kept her shoes. There she would find the ring that had fallen into one of her shoes.

An exalted Mildred called me back almost immediately to report success, and then asked if I would do a similar favor for one of her friends.

"Mildred, I am *not* in the business," I said.

Disney Slips Me a "Mickey"

When you read or hear the words "Disney Studios," you automatically think of the "Disney Magic," that is, Mickey Mouse, Minnie, Pluto, Snow White, and the numerous other animated characters who will live down through the ages. However, when I look back at my first encounter with this celebrated studio of "Magic," I cringe. Here's why.

I had been in Hollywood only a short while and was working hard at my job. Toiling in "La La Land" was an entirely new experience and one which, though demanding, was proving to be most delightful. For example, there was my introduction to the vivacious Peggy.

Peggy worked for Disney in the promotion department, and she was a true doll in every sense of the word. We got along famously throughout our periodic dating. So much so that one night she invited me to escort her to a costume dinner party hosted by Disney Studios.

Being somewhat of a procrastinator, I waited until the last minute to obtain a costume. Then panic hit. Where do I go? How do I get a costume?

But then, out of the blue, this great idea struck me. I drove down to the end of the block to the Texaco Station where I had been buying gasoline regularly and, after a bit of determined persuasion, borrowed the attendant's uniform.

Peggy and I made our grand entrance into the ballroom that night, amidst glances of curiosity and amusement. Frankly, I couldn't figure out our rather strange reception.

Anyway, while Peggy glided over to say hello to her boss and his wife, I drifted over to the bar for something stimulating. I had only been at the bar for a second or two when suddenly, four big

musclemen surrounded me and ushered me into the
men's room. Once inside, the "boys" really worked
me over, until I broke free and ran for the door.

Peggy was waiting for me outside and immediately took me to a side room off the ballroom floor,
where I barely uttered the word, "Why?"

She explained Disney Studios was having some
very nasty problems with a rival union and my
Texaco uniform represented the enemy. Hence,
the beating.

In order to alleviate any further bodily harm or
injury, Peggy lettered a little sign, which she at-
tached to the back of my shirt. It read, "Hands off!
He's a Guest." Battered, but unbowed, I struggled
through the remainder of the evening.

So went my first encounter with the "Magic" of
Disney. As far as I was concerned, it was more like
an encounter with Godzilla or Frankenstein.

We Didn't Take the Bait

The day was perfect for an outing. Perfect in every way. The Los Angeles area was drenched in sunshine. A wistful breeze gently swayed the palm trees. My beautiful date Von and I were looking forward to spending a weekend with movie bigwig Ira in his lush Hollywood Hills mansion.

Ira and I had been friends for several years. Even after he made it big in the movie business, we still maintained communication with each other; hence, his invitation to spend a weekend enjoying the amenities of his palatial surroundings

We arrived early in the afternoon. It wasn't long before Ira, his gorgeous girlfriend, Cindy, and Von and I were frolicking in the pool. Cocktails and hors d'oeuvres were in abundance. It appeared this was going to be a weekend we would long remember. Little did we know.

Following a gourmet dinner on the patio and

after-dinner drinks, Ira came up with the big suggestion: "Let's switch dates and adjourn to our respective bedrooms."

Needless to say, this caught my friend Von and me completely by surprise.

"I want to go home," I whispered.

In a flash Von replied, "I want to go home, too, *now*," she said emphatically.

Ira was adamant about switching partners, saying we had accepted his hospitality, and now it was time to play along and have some *real* fun.

At the first opportunity, when Ira left the room, we surreptitiously departed. On our way back to Los Angeles, Von was very quiet. I knew she was seething. I had never seen her this irritated. Somehow, I knew she was trying to figure out a way to get back at Ira.

By this time we were at the wharf. Suddenly, Von found the answer. We stopped the car, walked down to the pier, and purchased two rather large live fish and a bucket of water.

Back to the Hollywood Hills we drove and proceeded to park the car out of sight from Ira's home. Sneaking through the open gate and negotiating a myriad of flower beds and bushes, we arrived at the far end of the pool where we silently released the two rather large fish. Von and I wished them well as they cavorted in their new habitat of filtered water and chlorine.

We returned to the car and sped away in record time. What a feeling of smug retribution we enjoyed driving back to Los Angeles!

That was the last time I saw or talked to Ira. To this day I've often wondered if he ever found two other "poor fish" to play along with his sexual shenanigans.

Indecent Exposure

I was associated with the Charles Stores that had a store in Knoxville, Tennessee, where there was little to do for entertainment during the week and still less on Sunday. I had a good friend and usually spent Sundays with him. Many weekends we took Coca-Cola® bottles, and armed with guns, threw the bottles into the river. Our challenge was to sink the bottles by shooting the caps off.

One Sunday, for the sake of change and having no other plans, I rented a rowboat to take a solo spin out on the river. I was wearing a tee-shirt and swim trunks when I started. However, the sun was so bright and inviting, I decided to take a sunbath. Consequently, I removed my attire. I was tired from rowing and, enjoying my sunbath, I fell asleep.

I was awakened by the Coast Guard who gave me a hostile reception and charged me with indecent exposure and reckless rowing. I was stunned.

They were furious because they had been advised by an excursion boat that all the boat's passengers saw a dead man with no clothes on, lying at the bottom of a rowboat. I was further advised that the river was no place to get caught napping.

P.S. The judge put me on probation.

A Horse Laugh for a Star

One friendship I enjoyed during my time in Hollywood was the one I had with George Raft, the movie star. He was indeed a colorful character, and we had fun together.

George owned a stable of racing horses. On this day he had one running at Santa Anita and invited me to go along. That day he had a date with the gorgeous movie queen, Betty Grable, and arranged for me to escort her stand-in as my date.

We arrived at George's box at Santa Anita, and George immediately warned us *not* to bet on his horse that, according to him, was "a real dog." He had nothing good to say about the horse, so this immediately told the little voice within me to bet it to win.

You guessed it. The horse came in first, and George hit the ceiling. He wanted to know why the damned trainer had not advised him of the horse's potential and why he hadn't seen the "numbers." Quite simply, George was *hot!*

After he calmed down a bit, he quietly asked if any of us had bet on the horse? I sheepishly raised my hand and George broke out laughing. His only comment was, "Every dog has his day."

Frankly, I was at a loss to figure out just how he meant that remark. Did he mean me or the horse?

Finders Are Not Always Keepers

My housekeeper, Jesse, is a very special person. Besides being a minister—with a congregation of six to eight persons—for 38 years, she has been a valued member of our family.

One spring day I was preparing for a trip. I went to the bank and withdrew $1000 in cash. Then the question was, "Where—in a New York apartment— does one hide ten $100 bills?" My solution was to place the bills in the bottom of the filler of a moth-ball can.

Weeks later, Jesse advised me that this was the time that my late wife, Ruth, always had "done the closets," replenishing the mothball cans with fresh fillers.

I instructed Jesse to buy new fillers, replace the old with the new, and throw out the old—forgetting completely about hiding the money.

Several days later when I came home, I found ten $100 bills waiting for me on my pillow with a note saying, "I didn't know where to put these for you, so I left them here."

Saved by a "Belle"

Although many of my little incidents have taken place on the West Coast, I do have an amusing story that took place in Boston. I can't help but smile as I remember it.

I was driving down a large boulevard. Ahead of me was an elderly couple riding in a big car, which was zigzagging so much I couldn't believe it.

We finally pulled up to a traffic light, and I drove alongside the offending car. In no uncertain terms, I reprimanded the old man for his lack of driving expertise. Both of the occupants in the offending car stared straight ahead without comment.

The light changed to green and I took off like a big bird, leaving the old couple in the dust. But, I hadn't gotten far before a black and white car with a red flashing light pulled me over to the curb. The officer cited me for tailgating the old couple and asked for identification that I quickly produced.

After reviewing my documents, the officer reached for his ticket book. Just then, the old couple pulled up beside us, and the lady stepped out of the car. She confronted the patrolman and suggested he put away his ticket book. She told him to look at the license on their car. Lo and behold, the license plate identified the driver of the car as the Police Commissioner of Boston.

With that, the lovely lady advised me to be on my way and promised that her husband would sharpen his driving skills. You should have seen the face on the poor cop as he made his way back to his vehicle.

The Team That Never Was

Ted Kaufmann, who had an advertising agency in New York, was a valued friend of mine. At one time, we shared a common problem—difficulty arranging appointments with prospective clients. To get to our prospects, we had to first get through the secretaries who were powerful gatekeepers.

We decided to promote a women's football team for advertising agencies. We visited the secretaries to discuss their participation on the team. We asked their height, their weight, the position they would like to play, and so forth.

Shortly thereafter, the team was given a write-up in *Advertising Age,* mentioning, of course, that Ted and I were the sponsors. As a result, we received easy entrée into *any* executive's office we wanted to reach.

The team never played a game. We could never locate an opponent. But that didn't matter. We dissolved the team graciously. Mission accomplished!

Ruth "Cops" Out

If you knew my wife, Ruth, you were aware that she was one strong and vibrant woman. She had the tenacity of a pit bull, and, when she got on your tail, she didn't let go.

Such was the matter of my driving. I don't care how slow I was driving, for Ruth it was always "too fast." Bless her heart, she continually admonished me for my heavy foot on the gas pedal.

We were in the Miami, Florida, area on a four-lane highway for our honeymoon. I was driving down a boulevard in the suburbs, proceeding no more than fifteen or twenty miles an hour when we came upon a school zone. The speed limit was posted at "8 miles per hour." Again, Ruth was yakking about my rate of speed when, as fate would have it, a motorcycle patrolman pulled me over.

I immediately offered my driver's license and identification. As the officer studied the two, Ruth

Jack's beloved wife, Ruth Gutman

leaned over to the driver's side window. She told the patrolman I was "always driving too fast." She explained that she had warned me, but to no avail. Since I wouldn't listen to her, "a ticket would teach me a lesson."

With that, the officer returned my credentials, closed his ticket book and remarked, "Buddy. I know what you you're going through. You have a bigger problem. Forget the ticket." With that, he got back on his motorcycle and drove away.

Bless that officer. I'll never forget him. What a problem solver he turned out to be! I often wondered what his wife must have been like.

The Car That Came Back

It was Christmas Day. Ruth and I went to my mother-in-law's apartment at 71st Street and Park Avenue for Christmas dinner. My whole car was filled with presents that I had yet to deliver. We parked the car in front of an embassy about half a block away. We all enjoyed a pleasant Christmas dinner together.

Sometime later, upon returning to the spot where I had parked the car, I discovered that the car was gone! We dutifully reported the theft to the police. For a week, there was no word.

Then one night, I had dream. In my dream I was told that the next day at 3PM, I should go back to the space from which the car had been stolen, and the car would be there.

I followed the instructions. At 3PM, I went back to the space where the car was stolen, and there it was! It was covered with heavy black soot, as if it was fresh from a coalmine. It was a mess!

But, much to my surprise and amazement, not one package had been disturbed! The gas tank that had been full when I left the car, was completely empty.

Thinking that the thief was connected in some way with the embassy, I called the police and asked them to check the embassy records. They refused, saying that the car had been returned with all the gifts. As far as they were concerned, the case was wiped from their records.

Fearing running out of gas, I asked the police to follow me back to my garage at 77th Street. They begrudgingly agreed. By the time I got to the garage elevator, the tank was bone dry. My guess was that there had been just enough gas to travel to a coal mine in Pennsylvania and return. If I'd left my Christmas stocking, maybe there'd have been a lump of coal inside.

Love Those Texans

Don't get me wrong—I like Texans. They're brash, they're funny, they're real people, and they are proud to be natives of the "Great State of Texas." No other state in our union can instill the loyalty of its people more than the Lone Star State. It's an in-bred trait, and God bless them for it.

I guess it's because of these attributes I always found it fun to joke with and tease Texans. It made life a bit more enjoyable and zestful.

My career in Los Angeles had taken on a new di-rection. I was now engaged in promotional work. Through this endeavor, I had the opportunity to meet and work with several "stars" of the enter-tainment industry. One of my clients was the well-known bandleader, Phil Harris. Those of *my* gener-ation probably remember him. Not only was he famous for his band and music, but he was also the husband of screen star Alice Faye.

It wasn't long after I started working with Phil that he invited me to bring a date for a night of dinner and dancing at the Roosevelt Hotel, where he was currently playing with his hit band. I quickly accepted the invitation. I called my girl to give her the news. We agreed to meet at the entrance of the Roosevelt Ballroom, since she worked on the opposite side of Los Angeles.

That night I arrived a bit early and was standing near the maître'd's station awaiting the arrival of my lady. I hasten to point out I was regally attired in a blue blazer with brass buttons and white flannel slacks.

Suddenly, four "shoot-em-up" Texans appeared on the scene. You could easily tell they were primed for a good time, because they looked pretty "primed" already—if you know what I mean.

Seeing me standing at the maître'd's station and decked out like the Prince of Wales, the Texans naturally concluded I was the maître'd and demanded the best table in the room.

Since the head honcho was nowhere to be found,

I decided to have some fun and led the four Texans directly to ringside, which appeared to be the best table available. Once seated, one of the four cowboys reached in his pocket, pulled out a wad of bills, and planted quite a few in my hand. I quickly returned the money, saying we were not allowed to accept gratuities—just the waiters and waitresses enjoyed that privilege.

I returned to the ballroom entrance and there, waiting for me and mad as hell, was the official maître'd. Naturally, he had every right to be mad, since I had preempted his authority and also had taken money from his pocket. He really gave me a piece of his mind.

Fortunately, my date arrived and, grudgingly, my adversary led us to the ringside table Phil Harris had reserved for us.

Now, the funny part. Our table was right next to the four Texans I had seated earlier. You should have seen the look on their bewildered faces, as they watched the person whom they thought was the maître'd being escorted to the best table in the house by an "underling."

You could see and hear the consternation. Little barbs like "How come the hired help gets the royal treatment?" In Texas, "Cowboys get the bunkhouse not the ranchhouse,"—"it ain't like this in Texas," and "These Californians are flaky people."

Long live Texas!

I Gave a Hoot

A chauffeur from the garage where I kept my car struck a gigantic hoot owl. Knowing I worked in a zoo, the next day he brought the wounded animal to me.

I took the animal to the vet who made a splint for one wing. Then I took my latest acquisition to his new home—a huge, barn-like shed where all the food for the animals in the zoo was stored. It had width-wise crossbeams to support the roof. The owl with one wing flailing flew up and made his new home in the rafters.

I brought him food and water daily. After I had gone a respectful distance away, he would flap his way down to eat and drink.

One day, a month or more after his rescue, my friend greeted me with a talon-like grip on my shoulder. From that time on, whenever I came in, he resumed his perch atop my shoulder.

Eventually, the wing healed. After much debate, the head keeper, George, and his assistant, Wally, decided to give the recovered patient his choice.

I Gave a Hoot

We took the owl outside. At first, he flew a small circuit, then a larger one. The third time, as if to say "thank you," he flew around us, then took off into the wild blue yonder.

I had grown quite fond of this character and the funny way he showed his appreciation.

I *did* give a hoot for my owl friend.

The Baseball Coach Who Knew Nothing About Baseball

My sister, Freda, and I were the best of friends. My sister taught at a public school in the Woodbury section of Baltimore—one of the toughest sections of the city. I was a senior at The Friends School in another section of the city.

One day, Freda asked if I could teach her to play baseball in two days? She added that she had bought an excellent book on the subject. I said I would try.

It seems that although the school had talented student athletes, it lacked the funds to hire a coach. Since the school policy said that a member of the faculty had to attend every practice, and my sister felt sorry for the athletes, she volunteered to be the baseball coach. She needed to get "up to speed" and fast!

The first afternoon, I went out with her to the ballfield to help the boys choose their positions. From then on, she was mostly on her own.

My sister must have been a wonderful coach. The team pulled together and practiced diligently. Not only did the team do well, they ended up tying for the city championship.

Bravo, Freda!

Jack's dear sister, Freda Epstein Hecht

Flying High
for a Let-Down

Ah, Venice, Italy—the city of romance, magnificent beauty, culture, and art. What a setting for a few days of rest and relaxation. I shall always remember it, not only for these attributes, but also for an unexpected surprise with an unexpected ending as well.

Inasmuch as Ruth and I were preparing for an early flight home, I decided to check us out of the hotel the night before so there would be no delays the next morning.

Accordingly, I stepped up to the cashier's window and explained my plans. The efficient clerk was very cooperative and took only a few minutes to total my statement. I reviewed it, then gave him American Express travelers checks for payment. I was quite surprised when he stamped the bill "Paid," *and* proceeded to also hand me a fistful of Italian lira.

Now I'm no expert on foreign currency and exchange rates, but I was certain an error had been made. There was no way I should receive this amount from the travelers checks I had just signed.

I debated. Should I walk out the next morning with my ill-gotten windfall or call it to the attention of the manager and give it back? My better judgment said to give it back.

You should have seen the look on that night manager's face when I explained the transaction to him. He practically kissed my ring. He was both apologetic and grateful. He bent over backward displaying his gratitude for my return of the rather sizable error. He also promised not to discipline the erring clerk.

Early the next morning we arrived in the hotel lobby ready to take a cab to the airport. There, waiting for us was the manager, the clerk from the cashier's office, and two other hotel staff members who surrounded us to say, "Goodbye." To cap the reception off, the manager presented us with a very handsomely wrapped package. We gratefully accepted the gift and made our way to the door.

During the cab ride to the airport, we tried to guess what was in this expensively wrapped package. Could it be a tiny piece of Italian art? Could it be a piece of the world famous Venetian costume jewelry? We decided not to open it until we were on the plane. Our curiosity was getting the best of us, but we stuck to our resolve not to open it until we were airborne.

Finally in the air, our moment arrived. Ruth slowly removed the ribbon and then the wrapping. Off came the lid of the box and there, reposing in tissue paper, was the answer to our "high hopes"— a hotel ashtray.

What's the old saw? Honesty is the best policy. Oh, well, we shall always remember Venice, Italy—the city of magnificent beauty, romance, culture, and art *and,* hotel ashtrays.

It's on the House

"Sex sells" goes the old bromide, and I tend to agree to a certain extent. Hence this next little incident. It is a bit off the straight and narrow but still rather mundane when you compare it to the sexual high jinks reported in today's tabloids.

It was one of those nasty, snowy nights. The wind and snow were blowing everywhere. You could hardly see. It was freezing cold.

My friend George and I were headed back to Philadelphia and school where we were both enrolled at Wharton. George was my roommate straight from Kansas.

Somehow or another, we had managed to wend our way onto a backwoods road which was practically deserted, with no traffic headed either way. Still we pushed ahead hoping to solve our navigational problems at the earliest possible moment.

We started across a bridge when suddenly our sad old clunker of a car died right in the middle of the span. We managed to move it just enough to the walkway on the bridge, so that it didn't block traffic going either way.

It's on the House

With the weather worsening by the minute, it was incumbent upon us to seek shelter as quickly as possible. But where in this God forsaken country would we find shelter?

However, our prayers were answered when George spotted a porch light, just a stone's throw from the road leading to the bridge. Believe me, we broke a world record racing to that porch light.

On our arrival we rang the bell and waited with baited breath. In seconds the door opened and standing there in a maid's uniform was a full figured Venus whose total beauty caused both George and me to feel as though the pearly gates had just opened. Jeez, she was beautiful.

We stammered through an explanation as to why and what circumstances had brought us to this door at such a late hour, then asked permission to come inside to determine what to do next. In a very pronounced accent, French, I believe, the "body" invited us into the entryway and said she would call the "lady of the house."

Next came our second surprise. With a majestic

entrance from a room to the right of the entryway came the "lady"—a striking female to say the least. In fact, she reminded me of a character from one of Charlotte Bronte's books. Tall, severe black hair pulled to a bun in the back with a figure well preserved for a woman in her late 50's or 60's. But, most importantly of all, she wore a friendly smile and exhibited an immediately engaging personality.

George and I replayed our sad tale of car troubles and how we had managed to find our way to her doorstep. She readily bought our story and invited us into the living room from which she had emerged.

The room was something straight out of the movies—*Class A* movies. A plush red carpet ran wall to wall. There was paneling everywhere in either dark mahogany or walnut wood. The furniture was plush with hues of red, gold, and blue blending together. Heavy gold end lamps gave off a glow that complimented the entire decor. In addition, in one corner of the room stood a well stocked bar and a cocktail table filled with sandwiches. Oh, happy days!

It's on the House

The next half-hour was spent in idle conversation enjoying the many pleasures George and I had stumbled into. Our hostess was most engaging, and we thoroughly enjoyed each other's company. In my mind, however, were still the questions: Why was this "palace" in the middle of nowhere? And what was behind this operation? Were we going to be asked to leave or was there an alternative?

My question was soon answered. The time was growing late, the conversation wearing thin, and I'm sure our hostess was aware of the uncertainty in our minds. She soon set us at ease—and I mean at *complete* ease. She confirmed what I had deduced just a few minutes after entering the house. This palace was indeed a house of pleasure. Because of the inclement weather, there were only two girls in the house that night and no one for them to "entertain." She therefore invited us to spend the night in the company of the two "ladies in waiting" at "no charge," since we were nice looking college boys.

I looked at George and he looked at me. We couldn't believe what was happening. Here we were—two nice college boys who got stuck on a bridge, and ended up stumbling into this erotic situation. We agreed, "Let's go for it!"

Anyway, two attractive young ladies came down from upstairs. We were introduced and a few giggles were exchanged. Then we headed for our respective rooms.

I read this quotation in a novel once, "The devil got his dues that night."

The next morning, believe it or not, George and I were up early and anxious to head back to school. One of our "girl friends" of the previous night had jumper cables in her car, and she offered to assist in getting our clunker going. So, after a hasty cup of coffee and a roll, we thanked "Venus" for her hospitality and headed for our poor old buggy. All the way back to the car, I kept thinking, "I hope this old clunker of a car gets as charged up today as I was last night."

Anything for a Sale—Almost

Over the years, my career has taken many a twist and turn. Looking back, one of the most pleasant and rewarding periods of my life was the time I spent as a bond tradesman for Solomon Brothers, the brokerage house. I was young and energetic and eager to cash in on the big bucks available in this fast-paced endeavor. There was never a dull moment, and I enjoyed the challenge of prospecting for clients, then serving their financial needs.

Naturally, I didn't always throw strikes; in fact, I struck out more than a few times. For example, I had been trying for some time to arrange an appointment with a certain doctor to sell him my services. He was a well-known and highly respected professional man who enjoyed an outstanding medical practice on 23rd Street in New York City. His specialty was the treatment of venereal disease; he was acknowledged as the number one "clap doctor" in the metropolis.

I had telephoned him many times but to no avail. I could never get past his receptionist. Finally, I decided to take the bull by the horns and pay the good doctor a visit.

Immediately upon entering the capacity-filled waiting room, a very attractive young lady in a starched white nurse's uniform took me aside and asked the usual questions: my name, address, and other routine information. When she asked the reason for my visit, I told her it was rather personal, and I'd rather discuss the matter with the doctor. Very understandingly considering the nature of the doctor's practice, the young assistant concluded the short interview and told me to wait in the reception area.

It was approximately forty-five minutes later when I was led into one of the numerous cubicles that lined the inner office. I was told to disrobe and that the doctor would see me in a few minutes.

Before I could offer an explanation, the nurse disappeared.

The nurse returned and finding me fully clothed, insisted that the doctor would not come until I had taken my clothes off. Feeling as if I had no alternative, I undressed.

It wasn't long before the doctor entered the cubicle. He was a big man with silver hair and a ruddy complexion. In fact, he looked very athletic. But, he also had a no-nonsense personality. He got right down to business immediately and asked my problem. I explained I was not there for *his* professional services but to offer mine—as a professional bondsman. I said that I had called countless times but could never reach him.

He hit the ceiling. All hell broke loose. He gave me a tongue-lashing I'll never forget. I thought he was going to fire the nurse, who also received the same treatment, on the spot.

Oh well, I guess patience and persistence don't always garner their just rewards.

The Car I Hit on Purpose

One rainy day, on what is now Park Avenue South at about 20th Street, a car from the other lane skidded and was flying directly at me, traveling at a high rate of speed. Thinking quickly and wanting to save my own life, I avoided the crash by hitting a stopped car that was waiting for the light to change.

I immediately jumped out and ran to speak with the driver of the car I had just hit. "I'm sorry, but I hit your car on purpose," I said excitedly. "I did it to save my life." The small man, who had come out of his car, nodded. Then I hastily added, handing him my card, "But I will be happy to pay for any repairs to your car, if you are OK with that?" Before he could answer, I immediately said that he could follow me to my trusted mechanic's shop in the Bronx and I would pay for everything.

He paused for a moment to think about it, then said, "OK."

The Car I Hit on Purpose

Of course, I followed through on my promise, and as we parted ways, he said, "Here's my card. Call me at the office next week."

I called him the next week, and he asked me to come to his office. I arrived at the location on his card in an industrial area of Brooklyn, only to discover that his plant occupied a full city block. When I asked to see him, I was ushered into an office marked "President." He had amassed a group of people there and waited for me to be seated.

"This is the first honest man I've met in New York in some time. I want you to give him an opportunity to get our business. He deserves it." He was my client for years after that.

A strange way to get business in New York.

Meet Jefferson Davis Cohen

One of the most unforgettable characters I have ever known is Jefferson Davis Cohen. He was truly a lovable person. A millionaire many times over, Jefferson Davis Cohen was a man of the world with villas, castles, and mansions in more countries than I can count. His extreme wealth afforded him many luxuries of life, but his passion was his racehorses. In fact, it was my understanding that he owned more racehorses than anyone else in the world. Naturally, he owned stables throughout the world. England, however, was his base of operations.

I recall the time when he was particularly excited about a three-year-old horse he raised in England. He felt this slick-looking hopeful would become a champion throughout the world. It was his desire to bring the horse to America to start what he hoped would be a brilliant career.

There was just one problem. Jefferson Davis

always traveled First Class. He wasn't about to allow his prize racehorse to travel in the bowels of a luxury sea-going vessel. What did he do? In his typical fashion he arranged for the animal to sail in First Class accommodations. Believe it or not this horse traveled in First Class style on a Cunard flagship. Don't ask me how the sanitary conditions were accomplished. All I know is that Jefferson Davis and his racehorse enjoyed a First Class trip to America.

As an epilogue to this little story, the horse won its first American race and paid 19 to 1. But when the word got back to England that a horse traveled to America First Class on an English luxury liner, Parliament passed a law prohibiting animals from traveling First Class—regardless of the owner's wealth or prestige.

P.S. I had a nice bet on the horse.

(Please continue on. There's more of Jefferson Davis Cohen)

More Jefferson Davis Cohen

Another little idiosyncrasy of Jefferson Davis Cohen was that he loved to play bridge. He would play for hours on end, if the opportunity presented itself. But he was a stickler for payment at the conclusion of the game. Regardless of the stakes, he expected payment after the final score was determined. One night he refused to leave the table, until I paid him my losses of 14¢. He could get very testy.

Then there was the story of the night I almost broke his heart.

He was in New York on business and was staying in the floor-through accommodations he maintained at the Ambassador Hotel. The rooms were filled with his trophies, awards and commendations. In addition, there was a two-door closet containing a wealth of vintage wines and liquor.

We returned from the theater one night and since Jefferson had only a $100 dollar bill, I paid the cab driver. I was then ready to walk to my apartment nearby when he invited me up for a nightcap. He wanted to reimburse me for the cab ride. Once in the apartment, he opened the wine cabinet and told me to name my choice. Not wanting him to open a new bottle of wine. I noticed one oddly shaped bottle with just a few remaining drinks in it. I told him I would finish it for him.

A sudden pall came over Jefferson's face. He became sullen but reached for the snifter and poured my drink. It was delicious—a nectar of the Gods. But, why, I wondered had Jefferson become so morose? Then he showed me the bottle. It was hundred-year-old brandy—the last he had of that vintage.

We remained friends for many years, but that one night will always stay with me. The night I drank hundred-year-old brandy and caused a grown man to cry.

Still More of Jefferson Davis Cohen

It was a very busy morning in the Wall Street brokerage firm where I had been laboring for sometime now. The telephones and ticker had been going crazy, and I was up to my ears in the details of trading in the bond market.

Once again the telephone rang and I picked up the receiver. I got a harried SOS from our doorman downstairs telling me to come to the entrance "immediately." Not knowing what to expect, I made a dash for the elevators and the front door.

In no time at all, I was at the curb of our building. There was Jefferson Davis Cohen, wearing only a cutaway with a starched bib shirt on this snowy, winter day, gesticulating violently. He was going toe to toe with a New York cabby.

When I appeared, he started insisting, "Pay the man, pay the man. I have no money."

Finally, we dragged Jefferson away from the cabby. As it turned out, my English friend did not have the cash for the cab ride. I settled with the cabby who returned to his cab mumbling about the "furiners" who screw up "Noo Yawk." I steered Jefferson back to my office in the building.

Needless to say, he was very apologetic for causing this minor brawl on Wall Street, but I was not prepared for his next move.

Quite benignly and in a very low key he said, "By the way, I want you to place an order for a hundred thousand dollars worth of bonds. I'll give you a check." Can you believe it? Here's a man who didn't have cab fare placing an order with me for $100,000 worth of bonds. Knowing his reputation, his check was accepted without question. What a return on investment!

The strange thing was Jefferson then told me that he could never give me another order, because he, himself, owned an interest in another brokerage house, A.C. Blumenthal. He said that his partner, "Blumey," wouldn't like it.

That was Jefferson Davis Cohen. I'll never forget him.

Adios, Duncan

Living on the East Coast, I was friends with the woman who ended up marrying the movie actor Duncan Rinaldo, noted for his outstanding portrayal of Western villains. When I moved to California, I enjoyed many pleasurable days with Duncan, his wife and their two children. Unlike his roles, in real life Duncan was a family man and a loving father.

Duncan lamented the fact that he had no friends he could really trust, because many of the people in Hollywood were so phony he couldn't feel comfortable sharing himself with them. Duncan did choose to confide in me—sharing his most private thoughts.

One of Duncan's greatest frustrations was that he was too effective as the villain. No matter how many times he asked, movie directors insisted on typecasting him as the villain.

I was more than a little saddened when I read of the passing of Duncan. He and I had been friends for many years and, although we hadn't seen each other recently, the memories of the good times we shared will always be with me.

Duncan had a unique record going for him. He had appeared in forty-nine movies, including Hollywood back lot westerns, movies made in Mexico, and such action films as **The Mark of Zorro**. His traditional role was that of the villain and, not once in forty-nine films, was he left standing at the end of the movie. He always met his doom before "The End" appeared on the screen. His goal was to be left standing at the end of at least one movie.

There's little more I can add to this story, but I pray that Duncan will get his wish, and the big Director in the sky will assure him of a role where he will be vertical at the end of the movie.

God bless you, Duncan

Cast Your Bread upon the Waters

This was a night not to be walking your dog. It was December—it was Chicago—and the wind was blowing off Lake Michigan like a blast out of the Arctic Circle. Frankly, I was chilled to the bone.

However, it didn't seem to bother Duchess, my faithful pooch. She sniffed, she squatted, and pulled on her leash as though she was having the time of her life. Not me. I kept wondering if my body heat would ever rise to a normal 98.6 degrees ever again.

I finally decided we had had enough and headed for the local pub. I could see the Schlitz sign glowing in the window, beckoning me to come in from the cold.

Once inside it took only a moment's glance to see the tavern was practically deserted. Very few had ventured out on this freezing night, and only two couples occupied booths in the dining section. One stool was taken at the bar. With my appearance, there were then two at the bar.

We looked each other over but said nothing. I sipped my highball, enjoying the warming effect. At the same time, I became more than a little intrigued with this character at the bar.

He seemed to be a fairly elderly man with rugged features denoting possibly a man of the outdoors. His complexion was ruddy, and his gnarled hands gave further evidence that he was a farmer or someone engaged in outdoor work.

The old man and Duchess were fast friends. He was enjoying petting her, and she was loving every stroke. I finally broke the silence and introduced myself. He, in turn, told me to call him "Dad."

After an exchange of pleasantries and conversation, we got around to Dad's story—a quite bizarre story that would involve me for some time to come.

Dad was a native of Covington, Kentucky, and worked as a trainer for a racing stable. He had labored there for many years, until the owner passed away, and Dad became unemployed. His only sources of income were a small pension that the stable owner had funded for him and a small, monthly Social Security check. Actually, his income was a mere pittance, and Dad had a hard time paying for a boarding house room and food to eat.

Dad's one driving ambition was to save enough money each week to pay for a trip to Chicago. He wanted to visit his daughter, son-in-law, and grandson. His daughter's weekly letters to him were filled with glowing reports of their lives in Chicago and how well they were doing. Everything seemed to be going their way. That made it even more important for Dad to make the trip to Chicago.

Unfortunately, Dad did make it to the Windy City. I say "unfortunately" because what Dad found was the scene of a family living in abject poverty— a scene just the opposite from what his daughter had pictured to him in her letters. And, most unfortunately of all, his family could ill afford to feed another mouth at the dinner table. Dad immediately donated the few dollars he possessed, and now, there was the matter of Dad returning to Covington without the funds for a return ticket.

So here he sat at the bar—the price of a couple of beers in his pocket and no money for a return to Covington. He was emotionally drained and at his wits end.

Don't get me wrong. I am not a sucker for an easy "touch." My funds, too, were limited. But the fact is, Dad's story got to me. I decided I had to help this poor guy.

After considerable discussion, we got in my car and drove to the daughter's apartment. Following my introduction to the family, Dad packed his few belongings and bade a tearful goodbye to his loved ones. It was back to the frigid weather outside and a trip to the train station where I paid for his ticket to Covington, Kentucky. As luck would have it, Dad didn't have long to wait before boarding the 4:00AM train. In the meantime, however, he asked again for my address and phone number and promised to repay my kindness.

More than a year went by without a word from Covington. My chance meeting with Dad was now but a faint memory.

Then, one morning around 4:00AM, my telephone rang. The operator asked if I would accept a
collect call from "Dad" in Covington, Kentucky.
Though more than a little drowsy and feeling very
skeptical (my *father* was living in New York City
at the time), I agreed. I soon heard Dad's gravel
voice on the other end of the line. He apologized
for not getting back to me sooner but hoped this
call would make up for lost time.

He happily reported he was once again em-
ployed as a horse trainer. This time he was working
for a doctor who owned a one-horse stable. This
one horse proved to be a real challenge for Dad,
since it was anything but a healthy animal. The
horse had suffered a myriad of ailments that, at
times, had almost proved fatal. But, according to
the old man, the problems had been surmounted.
The horse was in "peak condition."

This "opportunity" was the reason for Dad's call
to me. He said the horse's name was "Crab Apple,"
and it was running Saturday at Churchill Downs.
He gave me the number of the race and told me to

play the horse across the board. Then, he said, we would be even. He would owe me no more money from his train ticket.

Naturally, Dad's call really piqued my interest. My only problem was to find a bookie nearby. The next morning I got a lead to a hotel near my apartment where I could place a bet at the newsstand. I left my $30 in an envelope with a code number on it and was told to come back after five in the evening. If I won, my money would be in the coded envelope. If I lost—no envelope.

You can bet I arrived at the newsstand a little past five. There was my envelope, waiting for me. Inside was $290. Good old Dad had come through and paid me well in excess of the money I had shelled out for him.

They say, "Life is a horse race," and I learned one thing. I really picked a winner when I played Good Samaritan to Dad. As far as I'm concerned, we both came in first at the finish line.

Carrying Coals
To Newcastle

I was alone in New York and my friend Mary was alone in Hampton Bays with her phone line down. A terrific storm had wet all the wires. Not knowing any neighbors who would be home in the late morning hours, she went out and braved the elements in hopes of finding a Good Samaritan. She was successful—finding an attractive young man with a truck, who checked all of her outside wires and interior phone lines. Coincidentally, he lived across the street, and Mary told me later how wonderful he had been.

When I asked her what he did, she said the only thing she knew about him was that he attended Southampton College. I thought it would be nice to show my appreciation. The local supermarket was having a special sale on a new beer. Nothing but a case would do—even though I had to get someone to lug it to the house for me.

The next day, I called our new-found friend and invited him over so that he could carry the beer back to his house. He thanked me profusely and could not have been more appreciative. We talked further, and I asked him what he did. "I'm a bartender" he replied.

The response left me "beery" eyed.

Don't Knock Wilkes-Barre

I had spent the weekend in Towanda, Pennsylvania, visiting the Ambassador to Bolivia and had enjoyed a most elegant Saturday and Sunday.

But now, as evening started to close in, I decided it was time to head back to Allentown and my mundane job at the variety store. It was most important that I be there precisely at 9:00AM to open up for a busy Monday morning.

The trip back to Allentown proved to be quite monotonous, as I drove the back roads with little or no traffic. The yellow ribbon in the center of the road was starting to get to me so, as I pulled into Wilkes-Barre, I decided to look for a friendly stop where I could rest for a minute and get directions to my ultimate goal—Allentown.

As you can imagine, Wilkes-Barre on a Sunday night looked like a ghost town. There was not a light in sight. However, just as I was about to give up,

I sighted a tiny beam emanating from a small real
estate office. Targeting this most welcome sight,
I pulled up in front, got out, and entered the office.

I was greeted by a handsome young man who invited me in and offered his assistance in any man-
ner possible. We began talking, and it wasn't long
before he retrieved a bottle of Scotch from a desk
drawer. Then things really warmed up.

During the course of our conversation, he said he
was waiting for his girlfriend to pick him up. The
two of them, plus a friend of the girlfriend, were
going to make a night of it at an after hours club he
belonged to. He then asked if I would be interested
in escorting the "friend."

Although the specter of opening the variety store
in Allentown at 9:00 the next morning was in the
back of my mind, the opportunity to have fun in
Wilkes-Barre with a blind date was definitely
more appealing.

And, what a decision it turned out to be. The two

girls showed up, each in her own Cadillac convertible. I couldn't believe it—two beautiful women in two beautiful Cadillacs. Introductions were made, and off we went to the after-hours club.

Take my word for it—even on a Sunday night, Wilkes-Barre is "something else." Things were really swinging in the after-hours club. The crowd was loud and lively, the recorded music was *hot,* and the drinks were aplenty. What a fun time we had! We partied into the wee hours.

Finally, my good-looking little date said the hour was late, and she needed a bit of air. She suggested we go outside. Once out, she took my hand and led me to her car. I started to get in the front seat, but she pulled that forward and steered me to the back seat. Need I offer additional details?

I opened the Allentown variety store promptly at 9:00AM, Monday morning. Things were under control. I had taken charge. At least, I hoped this was the appearance I conveyed to the shoppers.

"Variety" was the key word here in the store but, last night in the back seat of that convertible, "variety" had an entirely different meaning. Never before had I been called upon to be so agile, so gymnastic, or so athletic, as that back seat had demanded. But, according to my cuddly date, I had passed the test on all counts.

Viva variety!

Why I Like Roosevelt Raceway

Many of my friends are skeptical of my racetrack stories. One evening I was at Roosevelt Raceway and picked a triple—largely due to the fact that I had great faith in a particular horse that was paying 38 to 1—the longest of long shots for the day.

Based on this return, I believe horses are better than Wall Street. The testimonial you see below speaks for itself.

Jack's winnings at Roosevelt Raceway, December 10, 1965 $34,540.60.

Someone Who Watched Over Me

It was the month of February and I was enjoying a mid-winter vacation in Florida. Naturally, I hoped to take in the horseracing scene, so at the first opportunity, I hailed a cab for Tampa Downs.

On leaving my taxi, I was greeted by a dignified senior citizen who wanted to know if this visit was my first to the clubhouse. I advised him it was and entered the club house as his guest. In the dining room, I had a lovely young server who, after ascertaining that I was blind, read me the menu.

The next day when I came back to the track, a different person waited on me. Shortly after I was finished, my friend from the previous day appeared with a magnifying glass, hoping I could now read the track program. She advised me that this gift had been sent to my table by the bartender. For the rest of my time in Tampa, no matter where I stayed, she found me. On my final day, I said "Thank you and good-bye," to my new friend who had supplied me with the magnifying glass that the bartender had brought me from home.

I asked him how he knew to do such a thoughtful deed. He told me that the young waitress had shared with him how she had read the menu to me. On hearing this, he wanted to make my stay more pleasant. So I came away a double winner.

Jack at the track

Forty-five Minutes Out of the Way

Unlike other tracks, Tampa Downs is 45 minutes away from civilization. The local clientele all have their own cars. This day was my last at the race-track, and, because we had been invited to a cocktail party, I had promised Mary I would get home early.

I explained this situation to one of the ticket sellers, who, in turn, called management to order me a cab. I waited at the designated spot, where people who used valet parking also stood. After waiting an hour, I asked a stunning woman if she saw a cab among a large group of cars that was headed towards us.

She was kind enough to ask me if I was "concerned." I explained the predicament, and she suggested that I stay with her for a few minutes. Shortly thereafter, she introduced me to a handsome young man with so thick an Irish brogue you could have cut it with a knife—her husband, Eddy Murphy.

She said to him, "I made no plans for tonight, did you?" Upon hearing his answer, she asked him if he minded going 45 minutes out of their way to Clear-water. The woman, named Ruth, said she thought she could

Jack with his dear friend, Mary Covan

drive directly to the Safety Harbor Spa without help, which she did. Upon arrival, I asked if they would like to spend some additional time with me. Their answer was, "Where else can we take you?" I said no, I would like them to have cocktails with me in the beautiful fountain garden."

Ruth had been on the Board of Education in New York and Eddy had owned a successful carpet business in New Rochelle. They now lived in a home in Clearwater. We all had a delightful time sharing cocktails and conversation in the garden of the spa. Of course, I gratefully thanked them for going so far out of their way.

P.S. I also made the scheduled cocktail party with Mary, later.

An OTB Adventure

The other day I went to OTB, anxious to pick up my winnings. While I was there, I decided to bet on a few races. I was so excited that I was practically jumping up and down.

All of a sudden, the entire place burst out laughing. When I looked down, I discovered why. In my haste to get to OTB, I had forgotten to buckle my belt. In my excitement about betting on the races, my pants had fallen down.

I said to the assembled crowd, "Why are you laughing? You come in here and lose your shirts; I've just lost my pants." To which they roared, "Encore!"

Now It Can Be Told

Driving back to work one day after an appointment, a very unusual insight suddenly came to me, prompting me to pull over to the side of the road and stop. My mind was busy telling me, quite emphatically, that I was to go straight to Monmouth Park Racetrack where a black man would tell me what to play.

I drove like crazy and just made the last race. The car attendant, seeing my urgency, told me not to worry, that he'd take care of my car. As I went bounding up the entranceway, suddenly a strange black man approached me, handed me a program and said, "I have circled the winning horse for you to play."

I was the last person to get in a bet before the window slammed shut. I played the horse to win, place and show.

The horse won $34, $18 and $11, and I drove back home considerably richer than I left—even if it was on company time.

I Had a Dream

I dreamed one night that I would make a lot of money, if I bet on a horse named "Wilson." So every day, I looked through the racing form to find the name or any connection to it.

A little while later, there was a blurb in the racing papers that Wilson was bringing his stable to Roosevelt from Buffalo. He was in the area for about a month with a stable of about 10 horses. The public, never having heard of him, did not bet accordingly.

I played his horse on the opening night and won $37. Every night that Wilson's horses ran thereafter, I played them. They won six out of ten races. Wilson disappeared from the scene—never to be seen again.

Thanks for "Forking" Me

One evening while I was in Hollywood, I went straight from the racetrack to a popular restaurant called Mama Mia on The Hollywood Circle. I spent a few minutes enjoying a cocktail, then ordered my dinner. The food arrived in record time, and once my order was placed on the table, the help disappeared. No one was around for ten minutes as I sat there, waving my arm in the air—feeling very frustrated that my hot food was quickly becoming cold in the Florida air conditioning. I could not begin eating until I had a fork.

Shortly thereafter, a man appeared from the other end of the room bringing me a fork. He said that my ESP was strong enough for him to "get the message." He said he had no time to talk with me, but knew that we had one thing in common which was the racetrack. He asked that I look for him the next day at table ten at the track. I thanked him for "forking me."

Watch Out on Madison Avenue

I am sure by now you have come to the conclusion that my life has been comprised of one little "milk and cookie" incident after another. Not quite true.

It was a beautiful July morning on New York's Madison Avenue. Since I was near 56th Street, I decided I would drop off my watch for repair at Kobrin Brothers, a jewelry company I had done business with for quite a number of years.

Upon entering the store, a well-dressed young man greeted me and asked if he could be of assistance. I told him I would like to see Mr. Kobrin and would wait if he was busy at the present time.

With that, the young greeter whipped out a gun, pushed out the cylinder to show it was fully loaded, twirled the cylinder several times, and ordered me to close my eyes. Gun pressed against my neck, I was forced into a rear room.

The gunman then asked if my attaché case contained any jewelry? When I explained that its content was basically advertising material, he took my word for it but then asked for my wallet.

I must admit, the robber and his cohort were quite decent. They removed fifty dollars from my wallet but then returned it along with my credit cards and the usual billfold material. They even let me keep my gold graduation watch after I explained that it had been a treasured gift from my father. They then handcuffed me with Spanish hand cuffs to a water pipe where, rolling handcuffed next to me on the floor, were the two Kobrin Brothers.

They Took the Gems, Left the Bracelets

Jewelry store owner Abe Kobrin (left) and Patrolman Marcel Raymond watch Patrolman Frank O'Riley cut handcuffs off customer Jack Epstein. He was cuffed to pipe by three men who heisted Madison Ave. shop for $200,000 in gems. —Story on page 3

It was just a minute or so later when the young "greeter" thug reappeared with a lady customer who was immediately robbed of her diamond engagement ring and wedding ring and forced at gunpoint to sit in the corner of the room.

Before we knew it, the three thugs left with an estimated $300,000 in gems. One of the owners managed to trip a Holmes Alarm, and the police were there in a matter of minutes. They soon freed the two owners from the conventional handcuffs and tried to calm the lady customer.

But, with me, they had a problem. The only way they could remove the exceptionally thin Spanish handcuffs was to cut them from my wrists. This prospect was not a very happy thought since the wire was very tight, and there was very little room to cut the wire cuffs without slicing my wrists as well.

To add to my concern, the detective who was directed to perform this rather delicate feat was about six and a half feet tall and had arms and hands like hams. Near panic almost overcame me as I watched the wire cutter deftly approach the handcuff binding my wrist. I kept waiting for the blood to start gushing from my wrists. It never happened. In a split second, the "operation" was performed. I was a free man. What a relief!

Yes, it was a beautiful day on Madison Avenue, but also one I'd just as soon forget.

P.S. I had an appointment at an ad agency that day and called to explain why I had not been able to keep it. "These media salesman!" thought my client—"chained to a pipe—a likely story!" Just then his TV news program came on with my picture and the story. The newspapers' articles followed.

The Wrong Place at the Right Time

As a twenty-something, sometime in the 1930's, I moved to southern California, where I opened a new office and printing plant with a partner. This advertising and public relations office was combined with a plant that did specialty printing. Both were located all the way downtown, on Santee Street. I was living in Hollywood at the time and Los Angeles geography had remained a mystery to me.

One day, I decided to remedy that situation. I reasoned that I could learn about the LA streets by taking public transportation. I parked my car near my apartment at the Ambassador Hotel. I took a bus, so that I could watch the route and thus learn my way around the city.

I went to the office and handled the business that required my attention. At the end of the day, I left the office to look for the return bus stop. Seeing streetcar tracks and a sign for a streetcar stop, I decided to wait for the streetcar. I waited, and waited, . . . and waited.

About 40 minutes later, one car appeared on the deserted street—a large Cadillac. I flagged down the driver and asked about when the streetcars might run in that area. He let me know that street-cars hadn't run there in three years. Then he offered me a ride back to civilization. He asked where I was going, and when I replied that my car was parked at the Ambassador Hotel, I know he thought it was a bit odd.

When I asked what he did for a living, he told me he was "an unemployed actor." Although the deadline had pasted, I offered to "pull some strings" and help him get an audition for the exclu-sive, "First Little Show." At the time, this event was a unique showcase for the best performers in the United States. He took my address and phone number to call me.

Then he said, "I don't want you to worry about me. We own two movie theatres, the office building we're in and currently have 40 acts on the road." At that time in show business, the dance team Yolanda and Velez were household words. I had just met Velez.

Velez did business with Sam Lessin who was the broker for Schencks, one of the premier families of film producers in Hollywood. Velez called Sam and said, "I want you to give this young man an opportunity. This is the first time anybody has offered me a job in 20 years and I want to give this young man all the business I can."

Sometimes being in the wrong place at the right time really pays off!

The Best Trip
I Ever Had

I arrived at La Guardia Airport in plenty of time to catch my flight for Fort Lauderdale. I had my ticket and my boarding pass and I was sitting in my wheelchair waiting to board the plane.

I was wearing my Navy cap from the Battleship U.S.S. Iowa. A well-dressed stranger appeared and asked me if I knew how much the Iowa weighed. I told him, "79,000 tons." He then asked me about the firepower of the ship, and I replied, "Twenty-five miles." He then wanted to know the number of the contingent of marines that were carried aboard. I immediately replied, "Five hundred."

He said, "I have one more question to ask you: What was the name of the sister ship?" I said, "That's easy, the Missouri." With that, this total stranger demanded that I give him my plane ticket. My ESP said that I should, so I did.

Fifteen minutes later, I was wondering if I was

really going to get on the plane. However, no sooner had the thought crossed my mind, then he reappeared. He then made the following statement: "Your travel agent made a mistake. I have your new ticket and your new boarding pass—first class to Fort Lauderdale. An African-American male will meet you ten minutes before the plane leaves and help you on board."

Then my new friend said, "I have no time to talk to you. My brother was on the Missouri." And he walked away. Ten minutes before the plane was scheduled to depart, the young black man showed up to help me on board as promised.

The story could have ended there, but it didn't . . .

Once on board, there was a friendly supervisor who, to make conversation, asked me what I did. I said I was writing this book. She said she would be delighted to give me a copy of *her* new book that

The Best Trip I Ever Had

had just come out that day—on the condition that I would send her an autographed copy of mine when it came out. By the way, her poetry was delightful, as it dealt with planes and the skies.

This trip was truly the best one I ever had!

A Black Eye
for a Hero

One evening, I was taking my daily constitutional walk near my apartment. Feeling tired, I stopped to rest by leaning against a car fender at the corner. Concerned for my health, a man on a bicycle stopped to ask if I was all right. I explained that I was fine, just tired, since I was not accustomed to walking long distances.

The bicyclist turned out to be a former cop who was distributing informational palm cards on safety. His bicycle was festooned with two large orange balloons—one in the front, the other in the back. He said the balloons allowed drivers to see him at night.

Then I noticed something strange; the retired cop had a black eye. Consumed with curiosity, I had to ask. His response: he had approached an attractive woman holding a book on the street. He held out one of his palm cards and said, "Please read

this; then you can put it between the sheets"
(meaning the pages of her book). She misunder-
stood and threw a punch.

Some good deeds *do* get punished.

Optimistic, but . . .

I am sure most of my friends will agree that I have always maintained an optimistic outlook on life. Come what may, I have striven to view life in a positive way with a minimum of pessimism. However, I recently experienced an incident in which a lovely young lady really stretched my optimism to its limit.

Rebounding from a series of rather debilitating physical problems, I decided it would be in my best interest to undertake a not too strenuous exercise program. Along these lines, I made an appointment to visit one of the more fashionable health clubs on East 57th Street.

The club was located on the top floor of a high rise, and the doors of the private elevator opened into a lobby and a scene of luxury and affluence. An attendant greeted me and took me to the well-appointed offices of the salesperson, a very attractive and personable 22-year-old woman from Texas.

Following the amenities and the get-acquainted conversation, the young lady gave me the royal tour. We saw the swimming pool, the steam rooms, the exercise rooms, the jogging track, then the bar, the dining rooms, the meeting rooms, and the game rooms.

Back in her office, we got down to brass tacks. She reviewed the official rules and by-laws that govern the club, then reviewed the obligations of the members and the decorum which is expected at all times. She invited my questions, and the matter of dues was discussed.

The $2,000 annual dues didn't bother me. But, the $5,000 security bond did. She assured me it was an excellent investment and that when it was redeemed in 20 years, my $5,000 would be returned with accrued interest of 7.5 percent.

As I mentioned at the beginning of this story, I'm an optimist. But I fear I would be stretching it just a bit to count on redeeming that security bond in 20 years since two weeks from that time I would be celebrating my eighty-fifth birthday. I did, however, thank the personable salesperson for her flattery.

To Jim, It Wasn't Funny

If you are a regular viewer of the late night talk shows on television or have the opportunity to watch young comedians in the comedy nightclubs, I am sure you have noticed that lawyers and the legal profession are the prime targets of many barbs these days. Some of these barbs can be more than a little nasty; that, I am sure, rankles the legal profession no end.

I must admit I, too, am guilty of tweaking the legal profession, and once it even cost me a friendship.

I had known Jim for several years. To me, he personified the term "stuffed shirt." His background was rich in tradition and money. Jim was a graduate of the finest eastern prep schools with degrees from Harvard and Yale. He became an associate in a Wall Street law firm and a member of the country club set in Connecticut. But, to me, Jim was still a nerd.

Inasmuch as we were both active in volunteer and civic organizations, we continued to run into each other from time to time. At one of these gatherings I invited Jim and his wife for dinner, and he readily accepted.

The dinner turned out to be a fun affair with Jim and his wife and two other couples hitting it off splendidly, as my wife, Ruth, and I looked on with great satisfaction. Then I goofed. I announced I had just heard a new joke and would like to tell it for our mutual amusement. The response from the guests was "by all means." I stood up and told the following story.

St. Peter at the Pearly Gates called the Devil to complain about the restraining wall between

Heaven and Hell being down. He told the Devil he wanted the fence fixed *immediately* and to get to work right away.

The Devil told him to forget it. He said he wasn't about to fix the crummy wall. St. Peter then replied that if the wall wasn't fixed immediately, he would sue the Devil. "Don't make me laugh," said the Devil, "Where are *you* going to find a lawyer?"

I had no sooner delivered the punch line when Jim stood up, his face red with rage, and declared he took exception to my poor choice of jokes and considered the evening at an end.

Sad but true, not only was the evening at an end but also our friendship. Jim never spoke to me again. It was a tough way to learn a valuable lesson.

Almost a Hero

I guess I'm like most men—dreaming of the day when a circumstance will arise where I emerge a hero through dramatic action and leadership. Such an event did happen in my life, but the effect was blunted by the not-so-smart behavior of two of the participants.

It was a pleasant night and, after spending it in the theatre, I decided to walk up Sixth Avenue to my apartment on 57th Street in New York City.

As I neared the corner of West 55th Street, I happened to look up. To my horror, I saw flames emanating from inside an old brownstone apartment building. Fortunately, about 20 feet away from me there was a red fire alarm box. With great pride and a sense of civic duty, I broke the glass and pulled the lever.

Almost immediately, fire trucks and personnel arrived on the scene and sprang into action. A few seconds later, a fire chief arrived in a truck with a huge searchlight. Now, I thought, here is where I earn my "hero" status. I briefed the chief on the openings where I had seen the flames and gave him other details I thought might be helpful.

But here is where the not-so-smart actions occurred, that, to my way of thinking, blurred my heroics. The chief spotted two of his men on a tiny balcony jutting out on the top floor. The chief trained the searchlight on them and yelled, "Youse guys all right?" "Yeah, Chief," yelled back one of his men, "we're all right, but we ain't got no extinguishers."

Nuff said.

Honesty in the Big Apple

The hour was late. I was exhausted from a busy day, and had gone out the evening before. After taking a cab home, I had just sat down on the bed to go to sleep when the doorman buzzed me. There was a taxi driver downstairs who needed to speak with me. I hastily got dressed and took the elevator down.

The cabbie had cash in his hand. After leaving me and picking up another fare, he became aware that a bill that I had given him as a $10 bill, was, in fact, a $20 bill. Because I carry a special cane, he knew I was blind and he suggested I had not meant to tip him quite so generously.

Of course, he was right.

I was both pleased and touched by this stranger's act of good faith. I offered to give him a reward. He refused, saying that I had already given him an adequate tip.

Let me add that while this kind of behavior may be typical *outside of New York,* you don't expect to find it here in the city. On the rare occasions, when I encounter people like that cabby, it reaffirms my faith in the human race.

The Fortunate Fortune Cookie

One day I went to a local Chinese restaurant. After I finished my dinner, I broke open the fortune cookie and read: "You will be fortunate with the stars and satellites." I forgot about it until weeks later when I attended a party.

At the party, I met a well-dressed gentleman. When I asked what he did for a living, he said, "I'm a broker."

Being interested in the stock market, I asked if he had any favorite stocks? He then informed me that he was "not that kind of a broker." He only dealt with new issues and only "in satellites."

I replied that I didn't have a lot of money to invest, but if he knew of a satellite stock that he felt very good about, I'd like to know. He recommended a satellite stock with a certain symbol.

Weeks after that, I met a retired PhD. from Zurich who had given up his practice to become a consultant on technology. He advised that he believed that some day every major company in the world would want its own satellite.

I bought the stock at 2. Even with the beating the market has taken, as of this writing, the stock is selling at 3-$^{7}/_{8}$.

In the future, perhaps I should only eat in Chinese restaurants?

My 90th Birthday Party

My dear friends, Robb and Gail Rogal of the Rogal Art Gallerie, were at one time owners of a racing stable. Reviewing ideas for my birthday celebration, they suggested a day at Belmont Race Track—A Day with Jack at the Track. I took them up on the idea.

The invitations included a $2 bill, and the invitees were so pleased that they did not use them to bet. We had lunch, an open bar, and there was a tour of the paddock to see the horses getting ready for the races. Everybody bet; some won.

The Rogals provided a bus from Manhattan to Belmont as their birthday present. Mary Ryan, the public relations person for the track, took me to the jockey room and introduced me to the twelve jockeys who all shook my hand and wished me "happy birthday."

My 90ᵗʰ Birthday Party

The Rogals' planning made the day for Jack at the Track. They even had a race named for me!

The Jack Epstein-90th Birthday (Jack at the Track)
Purse $37,000

Belmont Park N.Y.
Daniel M.Vines owner
James W.Murphy trainer
Ashley's a Hitter 2nd

BOLD 'N CLEVER

May 16,1998
Robbie Davis up
6 furlongs time 1:11:3
Secret Double 3rd ©

*Jack at the Track, Jack's 90ᵗʰ birthday celebration.
From left to right: Gail Rogal, Robert Rogal, Robbie Davis, Susan Tofel, Robert Tofel, Jack and George Hecht. Track arrangements courtesy of Robert and Gail Rogal.*

Goodnight,
Uncle Jack

Once upon a midnight came a tapping at my hotel room door. Mind you, this tapping came at a time when it was still *safe* to open your door. It was a maiden in distress whose problem was being afraid of mice and having two romping around her room.

This event took place in the Cambridge Hotel, and the bellboy, who had been unsuccessful in capturing the mice, was going off duty. I was unceremoniously nominated his successor.

With the aid of a broom and two wastebaskets that I laid sideways, I managed to herd the mice into the wastebaskets and dispose of them. The woman's husband later rewarded me with two tickets to a hit Broadway show. My friendship with the couple continued, and eventually, they moved to Chicago.

Months later, I received a letter from them saying that their young granddaughter was heading for

New York to pursue a stage career. They had obtained an apartment for her in my building. Would I please look after her?

She soon arrived at my door—a beautiful, statuesque young lady. Her name was Sue. She was a 17-year-old musical genius who could play many instruments and had come to the city directly from a convent. She wanted a theatrical career in New York.

I got her a job at the Paradise Nightclub, a famous spot that was owned by a friend of mine, Neal Grantland. He, in turn, helped the young lady get a job with an act called The Four Red Heads— and of course, Sue promptly became a redhead as well. Taking my responsibilities very seriously, I watched over her like a young uncle, even to the point of insisting that she be home right after the show *every night!*

There came a night though, when the lady decided to stop by and see me on her way home to her apartment. I had a bridge game going with three of my male friends. It was late. Sue knocked on my door. I opened it, and there was this lovely young red head, replete with full stage makeup, looking very fresh from the chorus. My friends just gawked.

She said, "Oh, I don't want to bother you, Uncle Jack. I just came by to say 'Hello'."

"Oh no," I said. "You're welcome to come in and watch." And she did. Later, my friends nudged each other, and taking another look at Sue, announced all in a voice, "Well it's time to go." Sue sighed, "Oh Uncle Jack, if they are going, I guess I should go too." And she did.

For days after, those friends called and all I heard was, "If it's time to go, I guess I should go too," and then, "Goodnight, Uncle Jack." They remained a bit mystified and a bit jealous? Goodnight, Uncle Jack.

Appendix

Happy Birthday, Jack!

By Herb Hamburger

Here's to Jack Epstein, our grand old buddy.
(Speaking of characters, this one's a study.)

A gent whose tastes range wide and far
From the strictly conventional to the bizarre;

At ease in all settings both casual and formal,
He also engages the para-normal.

Should you choose to invite him to coffee or tea,
Be prepared for a discourse on ESP.

For here's a man whose horizon still stretches,
Who won't be contained by a few errant kvetches.

From Key West to Lauderdale, then Santiago,
He's just been all over, including Chicago.

Happy Birthday, Jack

With his pendulum swinging and the insight he owns,
He comes out ahead of the old Dow Jones.

He dowses to figure the strength and weakness
Of every nag running the Derby and Preakness.

Racking his brain from dawn to sunset
For winners at Belmont and Narragansett.

A guy who's full of ginger and sass,
And still has an eye for a pretty lass.

By now you surely know all the reasons
Why we call our friend, Jack, a "man for all seasons."

So here's to days of roses and wine
For a helluva fella, Jack Ep-stine!

This poem was written on the occasion of Jack's 90th birthday celebration.

Dowsing, An Explanation

What is dowsing? In the simplest terms, dowsing is an ancient, practiced art and method for obtaining answers to specific questions. It uses the human body, mind, and spirit, requiring extended perception, that we dowsers believe, is available to everyone on the planet. To become an effective dowser, one only needs a positive attitude and practice.

How is it done? Dowsers uses instruments that they hold in their hands such as pendulums, angel rods or forked sticks. After clearing the mind of any distracting thoughts, they focus on the target or question and receive indications from the instrument like a "yes" or "no" response. For most people, a clockwise rotation of the pendulum is "yes," and a counter-clockwise rotation is "no."

Dowsing, An Explanation

What do dowsers search for? They search for almost anything. Historically, water has been the prime target, and they find water very well. However, dowsers also find lost objects, lost people, pets, gold, silver, oil, minerals and treasure. They answer questions about personal relationships, business decisions, health matters and any quest where there's a real need.

Are the answers always correct? Dowsers are human. There's wishful thinking, fear, and greed to contend with and conquer. A good dowser can attain an average 80 percent accuracy, remarkable and certainly worth the effort. Jack Epstein may not always receive the right answer, however, he would know *absolutely* when he did have the right answer.

Nick Samardge
Former President
Norman Leighton Chapter, Manhattan Dowsers

About the Author

Born near Baltimore in Pikesville, Maryland, Jack Epstein has enjoyed a truly eclectic and full life, spanning six careers and one continent. Jack has worked on Wall Street for Lehman Brothers and Solomon Brothers; in advertising and public relations promoting celebrities and their work; in retailing for a five and dime; in advertising sales selling space for *Parents* Magazine; in manufacturing creating swatches and sample cards for the girls' apparel market; and even now, represents an art gallery that sells original Picassos. He's lived in California, Florida, Pennsylvania, New York, New Jersey, Illinois, and of course, Maryland. Jack earned his Bachelor of Arts degree from Babson College.

A great believer in pro bono activities, for many years he coordinated the advertising and marketing course sponsored by the Advertising Club of New York. Throughout his busy career, Jack has served as president and vice president of many local clubs and association chapters. He now serves on the board of Elder Craftsman, a non-profit organization dedicated to helping senior citizens create and sell handcrafted products.

Jack's interests are diverse as well. An avid fan of the horses, he uses his own unique combination of logic, science, and special gifts to determine what horses to play. Fortunately, he often wins.

For years, Jack has been very interested in dowsing (see appendix for explanation). He has used this special gift to help corporations find water and oil, as well as locate medical problems that had stumped the physicians.

Jack lives in New York City where he continues to collect and recount more wonderful stories that make people smile.